Driving down darker roads

By: Chad Smith

Every word in this book was written by me. No AI was
used for ideas or editing.
This comes from the heart.

To find more books by me visit:

www.gattaca.world

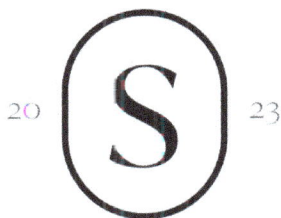

"I am just as afraid as you.

Enjoy every hug.

Life is short indeed."

- Chad Smith, December 2024

Table of Contents

"Those who seek life
shall die.

Those who seek death
shall live."

- Yin Sun-sin

"What I seek I cannot find."

- Chad Smith

"But, oh god, sometimes the Green Mile seems so
long."

- King, Stephen. *The Green Mile*. Pocket Books, 1996.

And I am here to break Dave Grohl's heart

It was on this road
blue shaking
blue blurs

riding on a bike

that I

down a yellow line highway

more blurs

became afraid

I am disappearing

more

Parts

falling onto the floor

red orange leaves

from a fall

October day

with a bit of musty decay

I would crunch up

scratch in my hands

floating away

Poofs

into the wind

I am a raft

floating

brown wood rotting

waves bouncing

no land in my sight

grey.

I wasted so many
yesterdays

and I

am all out of tomorrow

I am so tired of crying

and I wonder

when Taylor sat around

making all those albums

that no one cared about

except a few of us

does it matter

does it matter

     at all

and it must hurt

so much

     to still be alive.

feeble anger

you never lost your hair
but how hard it must have been
those bags of yellow chemo
as they poisoned your body

and what was then left
         of your family?

your big brother Chester
with his white house
and farm land he called
a garden
            watermelons
                    cantaloupes
                            strawberries

long gone.

your sister Linda
the red head always smiling
who lived with us
and taught me how
to count cards

regaling me with
stories of her time in Vegas
fell from her stove
         at 50
while making soup
dead before her body
         hit the floor.

and Buddy
who rotted alone in his trailer

it was weeks before
       he was missed
and found.

and George
who lived with that massive
embolism in his brain
just waiting to die

       for seven years.

and Eunice at 89
wallowing in shit
and Alzheimer's
       as angry as you are
            that she won't rise again.

and the children
       the ancestors
you shook off with your
bitterness
       and anger

dying surrounded
by your family

just isn't an option

       now.

And It's Best
(for my kid – Don't ever keep quiet)

I am living
  in a land of
    forgots

forgetting
  that black bird
sitting on a red rusted fence
  today

forgetting
  the mane
  of that Appalachian horse
    rustling in the breeze
  today

forgetting the curve
  of her smile
when I made her laugh
  today

and it's best to keep quiet

the father who
  never wanted me
    still doesn't

and I just need to grow
  up

but can you even
  grow up

at my age?

trembling in a tan vest
        full of explosives

I am waiting
        to walk into
a small square in Rome

where a man
        in a white apron
is calling out
        to European tourists
off the cruise ship
        hoping for a good
                tip

I am waiting
        to explode

I am living
        in a land of rushes

into grey

not black night (yet).

and I am breaking
        like colored paper
                wet on the edge

blown on
        shuttering apart

with my father's air

and it's best to keep quiet.

Sparty
Our king is gone

and the way
      I carried you
into Cleveland Veterinary Hospital

I took you
      to eat a cheeseburger
            before

you
      almost too feeble
            to swallow

we listened to our favorite song
      One For the Mockingbird

and you softly
      licked my hand

even then
      with the weight you had lost

it was hard to
      carry you

      cuddled
            in your favorite blanket.

I set you down so softly
      on the grey steel table.

when Dr. Thompson came in

all I could do was
          look in your eyes

hold you
          and beg you to
                    come back to me.

when I stumbled out

          I sat in my car and

                    wept

watching the dust
          grey
                    through
                              the windshield
                                        as cars drove by.

when you come back to visit

I never knew you
     with hair

but we were
     later
          in life friends

but you come
     back
     red and blue

and that laugh
     and smile.

you
     never stay long

"Hey bud"

and then you
     disappear
          once again.

I am afraid

on dark beaches around
the world
Fiji
Hawaii
South Jersey
the dark ocean
calls
for me

the waves crashing
higher
and louder

it is dark
out there

and it goes
into
forever.

Sometimes

I wish I had beat you out
and you were
stuck here
with your struggle
blues

trying

to
find
a
way
to
sleep.

On Letting Go

often easy to forget
      those times

too often
      not blurs

too often
      red and blue and now
           flashes
              snapshots

squints into a recent past

the lights always on
      too bright

eyes and masks
      block the fluorescents

concern or fear
I cannot tell

fingers move
      across my body

a machine screams
      I start to cry

rapid now
      an injection
           into the tubes
              flowing into my body

a new bottle
          glass and white
hung by my head

I feel my flesh

squeezing and leaving
          and cold

a winter morning

          blank.

Final Exits

deep sighs

coming off those roads
the bed and breakfasts
and hotels
were all closed

so we slept in the car
watching the Key Deer
slink across the road

you held my hand
and snored gently

and now
on these dark roads

I wonder
how many
exits
      I have left.

she's screaming
(when I stole the turkey leg at Thanksgiving)

I feel the panic off her
but
the house smells so amazing
and everyone is
together

I am ending

      my final laps

      my final days
           with my dad

I know because
      he keeps playing our song
"One For the Mockingbird"
and the water
      pours down his face

but I only took the turkey leg

      and all is forgiven

I Guess I Earned It

I didn't even
show up for
my own mothers' funeral

and in this dream
you don't show up for
mine

and here I am
        looking for you

beautiful and sad

but you are neither

only

broken wishes.

and holding on
to your wish
        poof
that I had just died
when I had the chance
all those days
ghosting the ICU.

I am

        ready.

I am fine.

I cannot

I can't
            I can't

and the roads
        these dark roads
whoof into the balcony of black night air

        another Smashing Pumpkins song on Sirius XM

I am sad
        and I am not

and trying to figure out a way
to hang on.

and I cannot sleep

        anymore

I feel alone

off
        in some desert
dry heat
and bugs crawling
across my feet

        trying to hang on.

Dear Katie

did you huff
any of the kerosene while
      setting your house on fire

could you smell it
driving away
Bright
on your hands

what did those orange
Flames
look like in the
      rear views

sprinkling off that glass
      off your new car

what love buzzed through you
as you drove past that graveyard
in Georgetown
where old yellow school busses
rot

      in the red mud.

And I am sort of okay

cold water
splashing onto me

as we brave another
     rapid

     Ocoee roars

my feet in black shoes
     forced into the green bubble
        of the seat in front of me

I don't want to be here anymore

I am sort of okay

     cold water.

The rush of wind

The next time
I fall onto the floor
I won't be getting
back up

further
and
further

away.

Northbound 35

I love you Richard Shindell

and when I walked onto your stage
at Eddie's Attic in Atlanta

with a note

from me

and you said you hadn't played

that song

In 11 years

but you would

Ii I could find the lyrics

I came on stage with my iPhone

and you spun into the song

as if you did it every night

while thanking Richard Foucault

Beautiful

and broken

and flashes

of your brilliant voice

      and walking up on stage

yet again

to hug you

will stay with me

Forever

or the short time

I have left

1am

alone again
no time
no one to
touch
love
a snuggle

all by myself

just another

time

"Why do people have to be this lonely? What's the point of it all? Millions of people in this world, all of them yearning, looking to others to satisfy them, yet isolating themselves. Why? Was the earth put here just to nourish human loneliness?"

— Murakami, Haruki. Sputnik Sweetheart. Translated by Philip Gabriel, Vintage International, 2002.

Coming Out Swinging

beige
  being
    beige

and silver caskets
  spray painted

like cars
  at Meacham
    auctions

and those couches
  always a nightmare
    green

a green of guilt

I wish I remembered
  tears
    and people saying
    how sorry they are

at all those funerals
  I went to as a child

but all I
  remember

    is laughter.

Ending Things and Hope

"I love you dad"

"I am just saying goodbye"

those two blue text bubbles

will always live
    with me

sometimes now just
    a blind panic

at 3am

and I am thinking
    similar thoughts

floating through
    black flecks
        of dust

but I remember
    your mom and I

stuck on a Ferris wheel

October orange cool night

the yellow and blue lights
    round

blinking

and she poofed
        ghosts
                into the air

and gently pressed
        her lips
                against mine.

The land of Meth

we used to call them
    dumpster babies

the ones tossed
    snow white
        into never

my last day
    the one that
        came in

with its skull
    shattered

it had missed
    and bounced

off the side of a big blue
    BMG dumpster

a spatter
    a spattering

of such a little body

all these years later

I still wake up
    at 3m

and hear it screaming.

Towers of Sand

death cards
from Vietnam

were supposed to scare

Charlie
Charles
Chuck

laying them down
on the faces

of these men
not as white as us

often now I dream
I'm walking bac<wards

through orange fires
seeing skin
searing hair

those smells

wake me up at night

just another war
to send little boys
off
to die.

Death Called

(and I stole this idea from one of my favorite books)

death called
      my iPhone lit up

light
      bouncing
           off the screen

and told me

the great black horse
      gigantic mane billowing

      was riding
           for me.

hoofing as she gallops

      coming

           coming

                coming

for me.

Grey Garbage

are you still taking
      those little pink
           oval pills?

and have you found
      a new reason

to suck them down
      with a side of tequila?

it still might be
      that body

we were just kids
      diving into a dumpster

looking for thrown away
      porn magazines

and that little body
      we found instead

smeared with grey garbage

"GAKK!!" it screamed

"FUCK!!" you screamed

hitting me with your arm

as you dove

    away

        from that little ghost.

The bone church

a pen drops
      onto
           this cold tile

as I sit here
and write

in the bone church
      in Rome

crosses of bones
      archways of bones

white
      bone
           cold
                so cold

as you are now
      we once were

as we are now
      you soon will be.

Oppenheimer

we were told
      so often

so many times

to be afraid

sitting underneath
      our little school desks

second grade

as if that magic

would
      save

any of us

      from the ICBMs.

Last Night

I came to see you
        you were so asleep

fast in your Ambien dreams

I sniffed your arm
        the way I always did

and snarfled into your armpit.

Then I wiggled
        into you.

I will
        always be with you.

and when we are together
        again

I will try
        to not knock you down

but my kisses
        will be nonstop.

A letter to Jesus

just like you
      I know
            I will die
                  alone

and those three days
      where did you go?

did you slay some demon?

and not that it matters

but not enough
      to hold back
            my dark

all that blood
      from your side

there was a time
      when I thought

it could make
      the pain stop.

Disciple

and sometimes
     I write in blood red ink

and it always makes me nervous

as if my forehead
     somehow
         zips off

then my brother
     walks into the room

dead for 45 years

speaking as if he
     were a disciple

he floats
     and descends

and I can only wonder
     if he is just a ghost.

The Last Unicorn

swam onto the beach
stood up and shook
off all of the salt sea
and then looked around

      for all his fallen people

he had swagger
and threw his horn
gleaming in the sky

after a few steps
into the dry hot
yellow sand
he began to fall

knees trembling
and when his face hit

      he sighed

         sand into the air.

Epilogue

"Tonight I can write the saddest lines. I loved her, and sometimes she loved me too."

- Neruda, Pablo. Twenty Love Poems and a Song of Despair. Translated by W. S. Merwin, New Directions, 1993.

Acknowledgments

This collection would not have happened without the encouragement of my wife Amiee and my TIRELESS early readers and editors Anastasia Smith, Bryan Center and Andrew Virdin. I love all of you.

About the Author

Chad Smith is a consultant and author hiding out in the Caribbean.